Fires Above Hyperion

Patrick Atangan

also available by Patrick Atangan:
Invincible Days, $19.99 hardcover, $9.99 e-book
Songs of Our Ancestors:
The Tree of Love, $12.95 hardcover, $8.99 e-book
The Yellow Jar, $8.99 e-book
Silk Tapestry, $8.99 e-book

See his blog and more at:
NBMPUB.COM

We have over 200 titles available
See our complete list at
NBMPUB.COM
NBM Graphic Novels
160 Broadway, Suite 700, East Wing
New York, NY 10038
Catalog available by request
If ordering by mail add $4 P&H 1st item, $1 each addt'l

ISBN 9781561639861
© 2015 Patrick Atangan
Library of Congress Control Number 2015943278
Also available wherever e-books are sold
Printed in China
1st printing September 2015

Check autopage for
personal items (most likely
DVDs) - patron George
Folkerts may have turned
some in with his borrowed
material & would like
them back.

Hyperion

angan

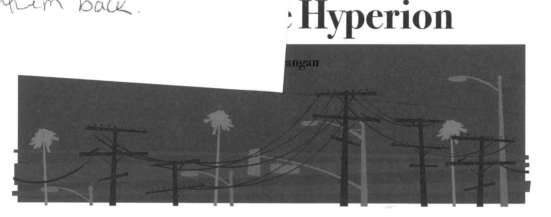

NANTIER • BEALL • MINOUSTCHINE
Publishing inc.
new york

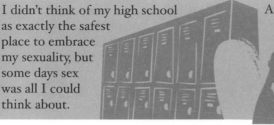

I didn't think of my high school as exactly the safest place to embrace my sexuality, but some days sex was all I could think about.

And as preoccupied with sex as I was, the idea of hiding my homo-sexuality was just as present in my mind.

The thought of being found out terrified me.

So I hid like a turtle--

--and got on by being happily undiscovered.

Like many closeted gay young men, my first foray into the dating world started off much like everyone else,--

--with a disappointing junior prom.

In fact, I didn't have any aspirations to go to prom at all.

I would have preferred to spend the night watching TV,--

--but I ended up reluctantly agreeing to go with my dateless friend Mildred.

I looked at it as an obligation of sorts,--

--something I went to simply because it was expected of me.

Mildred took great care in picking out her dress, particularly the color.

She ended up choosing a sequined fuchsia number with a balloon skirt and puffy sleeves.

It was hideous, but I was smart enough to hold my tongue.

She even went so far as to cordinate my tuxedo tie color to the fucshia dress.

"It will all look great with the pink lily corsage you'll get for me."

I have to get a corsage, too?

Unlike Mildred, I had never been much of a planner.

She dragged me to the dress shop and planned for prom months in advance.

Had I known what was involved, I would never have agreed to come.

I was always considered a safe choice when it came to dates for the dateless.

My looks were mildly inoffesive, I kept my nerdish tendencies well hidden and, although painfully shy,--

--I behaved myself more or less like an adult in social situations. Most important of all, I had trouble saying no.

But as far as Mildred was concerned, I was merely a minor detail,--

--I was neither here nor there, a safe bet, a seat filler, a cardboard prop for her prom pictures--

--which (not suprisingly) she planned in advance too.

"Package B: two 8x10's four 5x7's and 10 walletsized, all for $25"

My mind reeled at the skyrocketing cost for my share of the evening.

A $50 prom ticket, a $100 tuxedo rental, a $25 corsage and now $25 for pictures to a prom I never really wanted to go to in the first place.

As soon as we got to the prom, Mildred dragged me along and made a beeline to have our picture taken.

"I want to get this over with just in case anything happens to my dress or your tux during dinner."

She clearly had thought it all out. Either that or taken notice of how I ate.

"Sorry we're late. We went for our couple pictures. But don't worry, we'll be there for the group photos."

Group photos? You mean we are going to have to do that twice?

We sat next to Mildred's two best friends, Allie and Jenna, who wore coordinating dresses in different colors.

Everyone looked so nice. Even though I was wearing a tuxedo, somehow I felt suddenly underdressed.

Allie and Jenna were smart, pretty, and popular so, naturally, I hated them with a passion.

They all shared a love of choir. The three of them kept to themselves almost always clad in their letterman choir jerseys.

Oddly, Mildred was a completely different person around them.

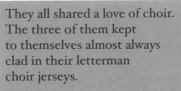

She seemed to mimic them a bit, not half as snooty as they were but certainly more aloof.

Allie was the type who saw people as a commodity. If she did not see you as particularly valuable to her, she simply did not bother with you.

From her lack of awknowledgement of my presence, I could only gather what she thought of me.

She had brought an older jock named Mark as her prom date. Like Allie, he kept mostly to himself, not speaking a single word to me.

Mark, older and from another school, was like an exotic import that Allie undoubtedly saw as some sort of status symbol.

I knew even less of Jenna.

From our few encounters passing each other in the school halls,--

--she always seemed to be sneering in my direction.

It was either open hostility or she had been born with an unfortunate sneer on her face.

Jenna had brought a friend from her choir group named Raul.

Raul was great, always smiling and just about as friendly as could be.

Like Mildred, I often wondered why he hung out with Allie and Jenna.

He also happened to be one of those brave souls who came out during high school.

Regrettably still closeted, I saw Raul's effortless embrace of his homosexuality as a personal affront.

So I pretty much steered clear of him.

But looking back, he was exactly the kind of person I needed in my life to help coax me out of my shell.

Mildred and her friends spent a good deal of the evening chatting amongst themselves about things I had never done and about people I had never met.

Even if I had been welcome, I was unable to participate in their conversations.

I had begun to imagine myself as some sort of alien to them.

It was a wonder we went to the same school much less shared the occasional class together.

So, for my part, dinner was somber and uneventful and just as flavorless as the woefully undercooked prime rib for which I had been obliged to pay fifty dollars.

"Prime rib? This doesn't look like a rib at all. Where's the bone?"

By the time dinner had ended, we all wandered off in separate directions.

I had lost Mildred, but had managed to track down the few of my friends who decided to come to the prom and we made ourselves busy taking snapshots.

But when I got back, the table was in disarray and everyone was deep in a heated arguement.

Characteristically, in the twenty minutes I had stepped away, I had missed something really good.

While Mildred and I were gone, Allie and Jenna had snuck off with their dates to take their group prom pictures together.

Not having anything invested in anyone at the table, I took it in stride. I figured it was me they didn't want to include.

I wasn't sure I wanted to be in the picture with these people anyhow.

Mildred, on the other hand, was devastated, openly sobbing into her hideous, fuchsia prom dress.

I stood there watching and wondered whether it was my duty as her date to comfort her.

I stood there and decided to do nothing.

She ran into the bathroom with a profusely apologetic Allie and Jenna in tow.

While everyone danced and looked like they were enjoying each other,--

--Raul, Mark and I glued our ears to the door of the girls restroom trying to find out what was happening.

Oddly enough, I was a bit relieved. All the arguing saved me the indignity of pretending I knew how to dance.

1, 2, 3, 4...

Should I be waving my arms or something?

I think I should be doing something with my arms...

This feels wrong.

By the time Allie and Jenna coaxed a puffy but now dry-eyed Mildred out of the bathroom, the prom was in full swing.

But the night's events had everyone in consensus that we should all move to a new location.

We gathered outside to decide where to go.

Mark, our designated driver, fished out a bottle of whiskey, most likely pilfered from his parents' liquor cabinet.

He then began taking veteran swigs in the parking lot.

Mark was undoubtedly trying to salvage the rest of the night.

He had most likely expected a grand time of eating and dancing followed by a night of drunken unprotected sex.

I both pitied and yet immediately recognized him as a complete idiot.

Tired and disheveled, Mildred and I turned to each other and agreed,--

--the night was quickly beginning to resemble a bad plot to an after school special. We asked to be taken home.

A few weeks later, our prom pictures arrived. Angrily, Mildred handed me only two photographs,--

--one 8x10 and another wallet size and cryptically told me,--

"I'm burning the rest. Don't worry, I'll pay for your share."

"But don't you dare give out or even SHOW these!"

When I opened the envelope, I immediatley understood why. There Mildred was in her hideous fuchsia dress, caught in an awkward smile with her eyes half closed.

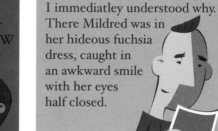

"I look like a deranged gopher!"

I saved her the indignity of agreeing with her by simply keeping silent.

On the other hand, I looked fantastic.

My teeth and cufflinks had caught the camera just right so that they sparkled in the light.

Fin

Secrets

By the time I started college, I was ready for a change.

I made a conscious effort to reinvent myself.

What many people don't realize is that when you are closeted,--

--coming out isn't necessarily a one-time event.

You have to come out not only to your friends and family,--

--but to everyone you've known.

It's exhausting.

But being in a new school presented itself with a unique opportunity to avoid all that.

There, I made it casually and plainly known that I was gay.

In college, my sexuality wasn't a secret,--

--it was simply part of my identity.

I felt liberated.

So-with my new identity, I entered college not to learn,--

--but with the intention of falling in love.

That's where I met Calvin.

Lucky for me, he and I shared almost all our classes together.

I used to stalk him a bit, strategically sitting myself near him in class.

Where, over long-winded lectures on art history,--

--I spent the majority of my time studying the back of his head.

It was weeks before he even noticed me.

We quickly bonded over our mutual love of food.

Coming out of a sheltered upbringing, I was introduced by Calvin to all kinds of new experiences,--

It seemed like so much of everything I was experiencing was new,--

--and I credited him for showing me a lot of it.

--from food to art to music.

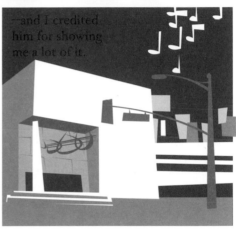

Riding in the passenger seat of his car, he had a way of making even Los Angeles, where I lived all my life, seem brand new.

It was no wonder my crush quickly turned into love.

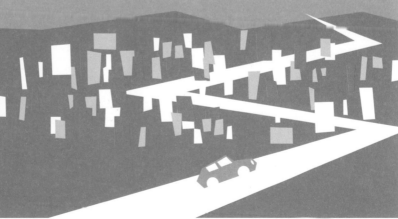

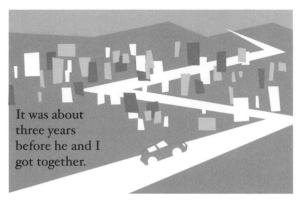

It was about three years before he and I got together.

And when we finally did, that seemed like when all our problems began.

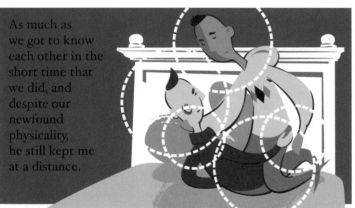

As much as we got to know each other in the short time that we did, and despite our newfound physicality, he still kept me at a distance.

In fact the closer we got physically, the more I felt him push me away.

Calvin liked his secrets.

He was closeted so he didn't tell any of our mutual friends about our relationship.

And soon I realized that I had become one of his secrets,--

--I felt like I was back in the closet with him.

Calvin was never comfortable with his sexuality.

He grew up in a strict Roman-Catholic family.

He once confessed to me when we slept together,—

"I'm not sure what makes sex with you so exciting, the sex itself or the idea of it being wrong."

This struck me as odd.

When he and I were together, everything felt completely natural to me .

He was always one of those rare people I felt at home with.

How could we share the same experience in two completely different ways?

Our relationship weighed heavily on Calvin.

And I understood. Life would be so much easier if we didn't have to keep our secrets.

"You know, if I had a choice, I wouldn't be gay either."

I think the words I left Calvin with that day, which were meant to be comforting,--

--simply added to his worry.

Within a few weeks, he decided to break it off with me.

Of course, I was devastated but I tried to be a good friend and understand what he was going through.

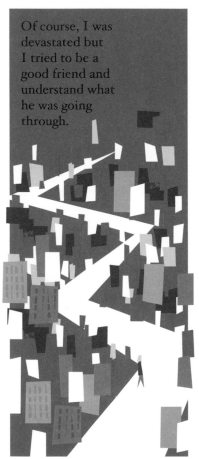

And to be honest, I simply assumed that he would eventually come to his senses and return to me.

But he never did.

And I didn't realize it until after he started dating again.

But this time it was a woman.

Oddly, thats when he decided to tell our mutual friends about our relationship.

And even then he flippantly said so as if I was the butt-end of an off-color joke.

"...Yes, I think they got married last year."

"Weird, huh?"

We were at a bar and had been discussing a former classmate's odd relationship with one of our professors when he blurted out,--

"You know what's even weirder? me and Patrick. We were together for six years."

Impossibly, I felt myself shrink

I somehow went from his treasured secret,--

--to merely a relic of a sordid past that he casually threw aside.

In all our years together, I had romanticized the notion of feeling a kind of pride the moment he would tell our friends--

--a sort of vindication for all the years I willingly made an idiot of myself,--

--following him around like a puppy.

I didn't think it was possible,--

--that it ultimately would make me feel like shit.

Why did he even bother to get our relationship a ??? it was only to ??? after it ended?

What was the point other than to humilate me?

Of course our friends weren't surprised at all. They had figured out what had gone on between Calvin and me long before then.

As I took a drink, I felt myself blushing under their stare.

??? as my friends scanned my face through my highball glass for a reaction. ???

I tried to pretend it didn't bother me, but I'd never been able to hide my feelings well.

And it wasn't long before my friends had an idea of how I was handling the breakup anyway.

In my effort to avoid talking to anyone, I had occupied myself with drinking,--

--and within an hour I had gone through four Tom Collins.

I was officially a mess.

As my friends dragged me out of the bar between their shoulders,--

--we spied a young girl in similar condition with a group of her friends.

"I love you!"

She happily wailed at us passing by, her friends holding her back.

"I love you, too!"

We all had a laugh.

But thinking back at that moment, I did love that odd drunk girl.

I was truly grateful for the affection.

Calvin's guilt about our relationship weighed heavily on him.

In our six years together, he had never been able to stomach saying those words to me.

I had begun to think that there was something about me that wasn't good enough,--

--that I was so unlovable.

And the way he casually outed our relationship confirmed to me that he never did.

But saying "I love you" came easy for that sweet, silly drunk girl.

As I ventured on a new life of singlehood, I couldn't have imagined a more timely way of hearing it.

Fin

GARY

Fresh out of school, without a job and recently dumped by my first boyfriend, you could say I met Gary at an odd time in my life.

I really hadn't had that much experience in the dating world and frankly found it all a bit terrifying.

So meeting Gary seemed like such a godsend.

I mean, what were the chances that he would be the first guy I'd meet?

Gary was beautiful,--

--He was smart, funny, easy to get along with, and most importantly,--

--and seemingly impossible to believe,--

--was that he was even the least bit interested in me.

Gary's beachside home was as idyllic as my image of him.

But as beautiful as it all was, something gnawed at me. I was ill at ease.

You see, there are two kinds of native Angelenos,--

--ones who seemed to be born swimming with the current, like Gary.

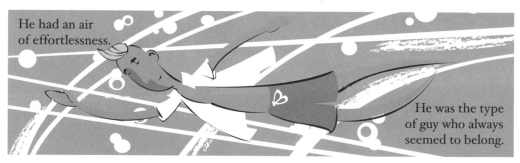
He had an air of effortlessness.

He was the type of guy who always seemed to belong.

Then there are the other kind of guys: the sinkers,--

--the ones who never learned to swim--

--guys like me.

Awkward and perpetually out of the water, I'm the kind of guy who would wear a sweater to the beach.

It's funny. In any other situation, had I passed Gary on the street,--

--I probably would have walked right on by.

After all, he's not the type of guy I'd expect to be interested in me.

But for today, anyhow, I was in love.

Coming out of a bad break up, I was in a really rough spot.

Meeting Gary seemed to be just the ticket.

And even though this had only been our third date,--

--conversation flowed easily and we connected on a level I hadn't thought was possible for me.

And despite our differences, we seemed to have a lot in common.

Coincedentally, he told me he had just ended a long term relationship, too.

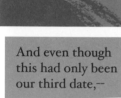

Towards the end of a long day exploring the beach,—

—we found ourselves back at his place.

I was just as awkward in the bedroom as I had been at the beach.

I hadn't been with anyone as good-looking as Gary. I was nervous.

We sat on his bed together for what seemed like hours,—

—watching random infomercials on the travel channel.

But I spent most of the time stuck in my head, trying to analyze the day's events,—

--trying to figure out if he liked me enough to kiss me.

I was completely clueless. It was a wonder how I ever even got laid at all.

But thankfully,--

--Gary wasn't as shy about that kind of thing as I was.

He took my hand into his and wrapped it around his waist.

And for a first time all day, I truly felt comfortable, like I belonged.

But just as soon as things were getting interesting,--

--Gary's boyfriend walked in on us!

I had no idea what was happening and all I could think to do was hide my nakedness like a turtle in retreat.

As Gary struggled to get his pants back on, I felt the little fleeting sense of place that I had yearned for all day,--

--(not to mention dignity),--

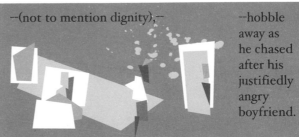

--hobble away as he chased after his justifiedly angry boyfriend.

But suprisingly, things only got worse for me when they started fighting in front of the house.

As I was getting dressed, it dawned on me, how was I supposed to get past them to my car?

I was trapped.

I couldn't just walk through the argument.

Who knows what could have happened?

And while Gary and his boyfriend argued outside with the kind of tenacity I'd only seen on daytime TV,--

--I was left with nothing to do but wait.
And wait.
And wait.

Too far away to really hear anything of significance, but uncomfortably close enough to know,--

--it had something to do with me.

I was in the ideal spot to remain as I had always been, painfully ignorant.

34

I never heard back from Gary again.

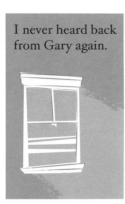

So I never figured out exactly why he cheated on his boyfriend,--

--or if it was just some sick game they thought up to spice up their dull sex lives.

In the end, it didn't matter. As I looked back, the once idyllic seascape had somehow changed.

Maybe it was the sun, or a thick layer of smog coming in from the valley,--

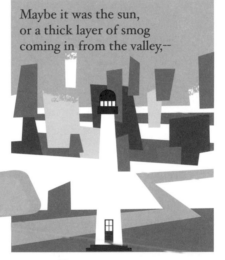

--or maybe my experience had removed Gary's romantic rosy glow.

But I was okay with that.

Oddly enough, I left happy, comforted by the very same feeling of displacement that had gnawed at me all day.

Fin

It's strange when you think of it,--

--but fire season in Los Angeles goes right through autumn.

The Fires Above Hyperion

It was at the height of a particularly brutal season when I ended a three-year relationship.

I thought melodramatically, as I watched Griffith Park catch fire, that it looked like the whole city was burning down for the occasion.

Even in LA where brush fires are common place,--

--it was odd to see one that was so large and so close to the city.

It looked like everything north of Hyperion Boulevard. was on fire.

It was eerily quiet for the peak of rush hour. I guess everyone steered clear from this part of town which seemed to be choking in a purple smoke.

I swear you could hear the familiar sound of flames crackling like a fireplace.

I remember walking from my car thinking the timing all oddly predictable.

Los Angeles is a perpetually youthful city where nothing lasts for very long, neither its buildings nor its relationships.

I guess it was the fire's way of telling me to start something new.

I had agreed to meet my friends Veronica and Roger at the Old Conquistador.

It was a bar near Roger's apartment.

In all the years that I had known them, it never occured to us to even set foot in there,--

--but the odd fires somehow inspired the occasion to try something new.

It was old fashioned and unpretentious, the kind of place that hung pictures of long dead celebrities on the walls and served cheap tequilla.

Roger was my newly minted ex-boyfriend of sorts.

I rationalized that with every failed relationship, I should try to keep "friendly" with my exes.

I foolishly figured that if I couldn't have them as lovers the least I could do was keep them around as a friends.

Otherwise it would have been a complete waste of my time.

In Roger's case, casually on and off for about three years.

For some reason, I saw this odd complication in my life as a sign of emotional maturity.

However, I would often end up with confused feelings that prevented me from moving on with my life.

Roger had recently started dating someone new.

But unlike the other times we had taken a break from each other, he was approaching this new guy with a kind of sincerity,--

--that only left me feeling jealous.

We tried to keep our friendship intact--

--but no matter where we went and no matter what we did,--

--it always turned out the same.

My selfishness was costing me my best friend and I wasn't handling it very well.

Veronica was Roger's work friend.

I guess Roger invited her as a buffer between us.

But I think Veronica had other ideas.

Veronica had been my one and only advocate. She saw the way I looked at Roger, even though most of the time he seemed oblivious to me.

But to her-- and I suspect anyone else-- my feelings for him were pretty obvious.

In between our sizable margaritas--she drunkenly blurted.--

"Oh my God, you guys should kiss."

It came out a little bit louder than she intended and left the two of us feeling awkward.

For a moment, it felt like the whole room stopped and looked over at us.

In between sips of his drink, Roger crookedly smiled at me with sad eyes. I think it was the first time he looked me in the eye all night.

We had a falling out a few weeks before and, from what I could tell, the look he gave me was one of pity.

I'm sure in his inebriated state he rationalized that it was an obligation.

On the other hand, I was desperate at this point and was grasping for anything I could take.

Knowing that this was probably going to be our last kiss I kept mine open.

Roger leaned his elbow into the table and narrowed his eyes.

My lips were sweaty and nervously stiff in anticipation.

I could have guessed that in my rather short list of all time great kisses, this wasn't to be one of them.

Because, despite my best attempts, in my drunken stupor,--

--I failed to commit any of it to memory.

The next thing I knew, it was over and all I could think of was that somehow I had been robbed.

Where was my last great kiss?

I wanted a do over.

We stumbled out of the Old Conquistador soaked in cheap Tequila, laughing.

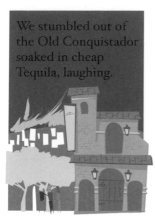

Roger's apartment was just up the street and as we struggled to walk up the hill, I lagged behind a bit, my stomach gurgling.

I quietly paused and grimaced to savor a stray flake of salt,--

--that once rimmed Roger's drink and somehow wandered onto my lips when we kissed.

I flinched, reminded of his response when I told him I loved him a few weeks prior.

"I never thought of you that way."

For the better part of three years, we had been sleeping together.

It was an odd arrangement for sure, trying to be friends. But for me at least, it was a relationship in all but the word.

And after three years,

"I never thought of you that way."

was all I got.

We found ourselves flopped in the living room.

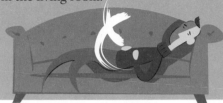

I selfishly laid across the length of the entire sofa cradling the newfound grumbling in my stomach.

Alcohol never settled well with me.

Roger knelt beside me in concern and gently placed his hand on my stomach.

There was a pregnant pause which we spent the better part staring at each other.
I realized he wanted another kiss too.

"I missed you."–

–I confessed in a blurry-eyed whisper as he leaned into me.

Veronica stood laughing at how the room was spinning, oblivious to us when she blurted out,

"I am so fucked up!"

–right when Roger and I were about to kiss.

It took us a while to sober up. But when we stepped outside, the air was heavy with ash. It smelled like something had just died.

On my way back to my car, I reflected on this odd day, the disappointing kiss and the missed opportunities.

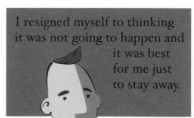
I resigned myself to thinking it was not going to happen and it was best for me just to stay away.

I licked my lips searching for another flake of salt,--

--but was saddened to find nothing.

Los Angeles is a youthful city.

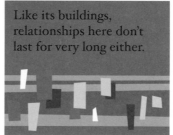
Like its buildings, relationships here don't last for very long either.

And every few years during fire season it burns itself to the ground.

I often think of the power lines that run through the city like veins.

They are the only thing of permanence in LA.

They connect
us to each
other.

And just about anywhere
I go, I am reminded of
these connections.

I can look up comforted
that somewhere, there is
a line that still connects
me to Roger.

Fin

I have this odd New Year's tradition.

I like to spend it doing one of the few things I do really well-sleeping.

It says a lot more about my life than I care to admit.

If you ask my parents in particular,--

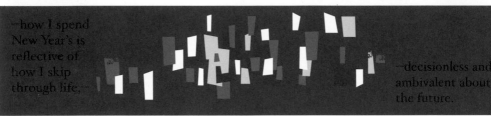
--how I spend New Year's is reflective of how I skip through life,--

--decisionless and ambivalent about the future.

I think the reason why I'm compelled to indecision is because--

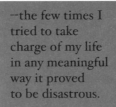
--the few times I tried to take charge of my life in any meaningful way it proved to be disastrous.

So to avoid disaster, I simply avoid decision making altogether.

48

But every year I am goaded by my friends to join them in the festivities. I think if they truly knew how little I enjoyed it, they wouldn't bother to ask.

But like all good friends, they ask anyway.

And every once in a while, I surprise both them and myself by accepting the invitation.

I've never been very good in social situations.

I lack the confidence to function in large groups like a proper human being.

I spent much of the party fixated on my watch, not counting down until the New Year but until the time I got to go home.

When I go to parties, I try my best to look like I actually belong and mimic everyone else.

I usually either end up hiding in a quiet corner indulging in too much drink or food,--

--or I end up cornering some poor soul--

--and monopolizing his time for the entire party.

I was looking for a quiet spot away from the party when I stumbled upon Essau.

Essau was a lot like me and much preferred to look down at a party than be in the middle of it.

It took me a while but I managed to fight through my many social phobias and approach him.

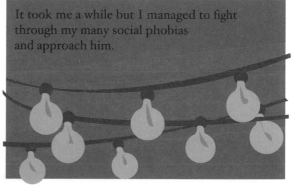

And to my surprise, not only did I manage to eek out a greeting,--

--but we struck up quite a lively conversation.

It turned out Essau and I had quite a bit in common.

So it is little wonder why within a very short time, I felt unusually comfortable with him.

Essau was quite the smoker,--

--throughout the entire evening, his hand was consistently adorned by a lit cigarette.

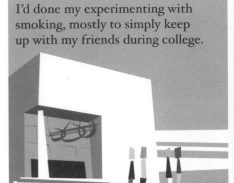

I'd done my experimenting with smoking, mostly to simply keep up with my friends during college.

But it seemed like every time I took it up,--

--my tolerance for it grew thinner.

So much so these days, a mere smell of secondhand smoke is enough to make me nauseous.

And normally I wouldn't even consider a smoker,--

--but everyone has exceptions.

Essau was mine.

And much to my surprise, when he offered me a cigarette,--

--I found myself eagerly accepting.

I think I wanted his acceptance so much, I was willing to become ill for it.

By the time I discovered Essau, it was already well into the party.

I'm a bit of a light weight. I was feeling toasty, having downed several stiff drinks.

And not having eaten dinner beforehand, I made a meal of what happened to be available.

Mmm... corn chips and deviled eggs!

Vodka and eggs certainly do not mix well alone,--

--and with the first cigarette I had begun to feel light-headed.

But it was something I was determined to brave through.

Something I tried my best to ignore as best as I could as Essau and I shared nearly half a pack between the two of us.

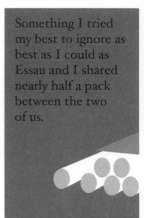

I can't help but feel disappointed in myself to willing to change so much for a guy I had hardly known.

By the end of the evening, I was forcing myself to smoke and with white knuckles, held back throwing up the deviled eggs I had consumed earlier.

I had already begun to taste them in the back of my throat.

I have a very self-defeating habit; usually the more attracted I am to someone, the less I am likely to flirt.

To be honest, I had no other intention with Essau but to spend time with him.

I would have been happy tucking the perfect moment meeting a beautiful guy at a New Year's party never to see him again into my memory.

I don't know if it was my lingering glances or something I said in passing that clued him to the fact I was gay.

But it was surprising to me when his tone suddenly veered awkwardly.

He began pointing out several attractive girls at the party.

He was not only straight, but for some reason he thought I was interested in him,--

--which I was... but for some reason I took offense, not to his very skilled observation, but his clumsy deflection.

55

Disappointed not only at having spent the entire evening with a guy that didn't even have the courtesy to tell me he was straight--

--I had literally made myself ill just to have the pleasure of chatting--

In my alcohol fueled, deviled egg fattened and cigarette clouded mind--

--my infatuation for him quickly turned to disdain.

I guess that's when I thought, what else did I have to lose?

And threw up over the balcony.

Luckily, I didn't hit anyone.

It was already towards the end of the party and the crowd downstairs had dissipated.

I didn't even remember hearing a countdown that evening,--

--much less seeing what must have been Essau's priceless reaction.

All I recalled afterwards of the ride home, were my friends laughing in the front seat--

--as I applied my protesting stomach to my throbbing head,--

--protecting myself from a rather bumpy ride home.

"Happy New Year!" They said in unison.

And I could swear they purposely drove over every bump and pothole just to tease me. **Fin**

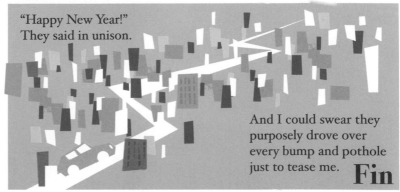

APE or the Alternative Press Expo in San Francisco is my favorite event of the convention season.

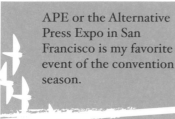

It was a casual event, filled with super friendly people selling funny zines.

Ape Shit

I always sold out of whatever I happened to be selling at the time.

And most importantly, it was the only convention that served liquor on the sales floor.

It had been almost ten years since I had published a book,--

--and I was itching to go to APE again.

My old truck had been on its last legs and I thought it would be a good idea to rent a car for the trip from Los Angeles.

For only twenty dollars extra, I got an upgrade to a hybrid.

Of course, I probably actually ended up paying fifty dollars extra once I calculated the fuel savings,--

--but I figured, what the heck! A Prius sounds super fun to drive!

I ended up crashing at my friend Jason's place. He lived in San Jose which was about an hour and a half away from downtown San Fransisco and the convention.

I hadn't seen Jason for over two years ago. Since then, he had a brand new pair of twins.

It was great catching up with him, but I realized the first of two errors in judgement I made in staying over at his place,--

--when I was greeted by two screaming toddlers at five o'clock in the morning.

The second mistake was that what I had imagined to be a brief hour and a half commute to the convention,--

-- had become a torturous hour and a half commute since I had been sleep deprived the night before.

APE was a lot different from what I remembered ten years ago.

The haphazard collection of tables of people selling photocopied zines had transformed into a slick sales floor of professionals selling full color books and toys.

It reminded me more of the early days of San Diego Comic-Con than my APE.

My publisher set me up to share a table with another artist and his wife.

The single book I was selling paled in comparison to the display they had brought.

I hadn't seen them in years and we had a great time chatting.

"Sorry I got here so late. Where can I get food? I'm starving! I skipped breakfast."

I had brought over a tall display rack so as to better catch everyone's attention.

But by the time I loaded it up with books it looked a like I had built fort and was hiding out.

I could tell from the first few minutes that this was going to be rough.

It was quiet for me most of the afternoon, but I didn't mind.

My friend Bruce visited. He didn't read comics but made it a point to drive two hours down from Modesto just so we could catch up.

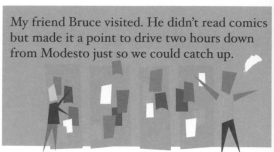

"Have you eaten lunch yet?"

"Did you see those lines for the food trucks? I think I'll wait for it to die down a bit."

Between him and my neighboring artist friends, it made the dull day almost worth it.

Needless to say, because of what I imagined to be the changing demographic and my idiot table styling choices, I did not do well.

"I sold one book!"

We all had a good laugh about it.

Towards the end of the day, I decided take a break from all that sitting to grab a beer and look around the convention.

That's when I met Bryan.

Bryan was fantastic! He was handsome, fun and easy to talk to. He lived in Castro and worked as a travel reporter for a local NPR station in San Fransisco.

In the odd laundry list in my head of the perfect guy, I had checked off the first four items;--

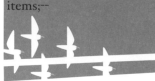

- ☑ Handsome
- ☑ Fun
- ☑ Easy to talk to
- ☑ NPR Listener
- ☐ Plays the cello
- ☐ Parents own a small bookshop in Berkeley and they don't like discussing politics over dinner

"Hey, I haven't had anything to eat all day! Do you want to go for a bite to eat?"

"Yeah, that'd be great!"

Within an hour of meeting each other, we had a date.

But first things first, I had to ditch my friend.

"I gotta go, I met a guy! We have a date!"

"But I drove down all the way from Modesto! I was hoping to at least grab dinner together!"

"But, but, but... Guy! Date! And he's really cute! Priorities!"

Bryan and I drove off to a nearby area to look for a nice place to eat.

"Do you think my bicycle will be alright parked there?"

"I wouldn't worry about it."

We wandered around downtown looking for a restaurant.

Conversation flowed. We talked about everything from fine arts to local politics to how much I like my beloved APE convention had changed.

San Fransisco had undergone a transformation that wasn't nessecarily for the better either.

"Yeah, things have become a lot more conservative here lately. You see more and more young families moving in.

"It's become more of a playground for the rich and a lot of the old quirky character of the city is disappearing."

It took us almost an hour to decide on where to eat and by then I had begun to feel a little bit dizzy.

We picked what we thought was a sweet little Mexican restaurant.

By the time our food came, I felt sick and couldn't eat anything.

So sick in fact, I had to excuse myself to throw up.

I ended up losing what was left of my apetite and merely picking at the food, which turned out to be pretty lousy anyhow.

But to top it off, it turned out the place was filled with families with screaming kids.

We were both miserable.

"Ugh, I hate kids. They ruin everything!"

Although usually I'm more tolerant of them, remembering my ruined sleep from the night before, I replied,--

"Awww, I hate kids too!"

I was in love.

After dinner, we spent the evening exploring the neighborhood and chatting.

But when we finished our date, embarassingly my rental car wouldn't start.

I tried everything, even opening up the hood on the stray hope,--

--that my mechanically feeble mind would be able to recognize something amiss.

"What's this thing that looks like a pokeball?"

We spent the time simply waiting for the tow truck driver to come.

"It will be about a twenty-minute wait."

So we waited,--

"It will be about a twenty minute wait."

--and waited,--

I was worried about the car,--

--and Bryan was worried about his bicycle.

He had left it in the parking lot of the convention center and didn't know how long he would be able to leave it there.

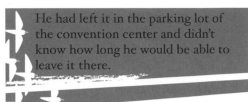

"You know, Bryan, this really isn't fair to you. You should just go home. I can take care of this on my own."

"No, I wouldn't dream of it."

So we spent the entire time in nervous conversation.

It never occured to me that we could have been making out the entire time.

But I think Bryan lost what little interest he had left in me by the second hour,--

--when I finally lost my temper and had a full on hissy fit,--

--similtaneously yelling at the rental agency on my phone while yelling at the tow truck company on his.

After the third hour, I finally said,--

"That's it, we are going to get your bike! The tow truck guy can just wait for us to come back IF he ever shows up."

Not suprisingly, when I told the rental car company our plan, all they cared about was the car,--

"You can't do that! The tow truck driver will be arriving in twenty minutes."

It turned out that the tow truck driver was really about twenty minutes away that time--

--because after three and a half hours of waiting since my first call, he showed up on our way back from picking up Bryan's bicycle.

"I see what the problem is. I run into this problem all the time with this model car.

"First, you need to press on the brake really hard, then the start button, and then the brake again,--

"--and then the gas, then press up, then down,--

"--then left, then right, B, A, select, and start."

As convoluted as his solution to starting the car was,--

--He said it in such a matter-of-fact way that it made me feel like an idiot for not already knowing it.

Even though I figured out how to start the car, I still didn't feel safe in it.

I decided to have the car towed and exchange it for another one, but the only rental agency open was on the other side of town.

It took an hour to get there and another hour and a half before I made it back to my friend's house in San Jose.

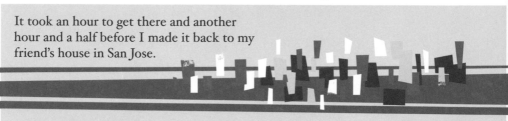

Bryan and I never got back together after that.

To be honest, I can't blame him. I behaved horribly.

But it was just as well, because I had to wake up even earlier to make it on time for the second day of the convention.

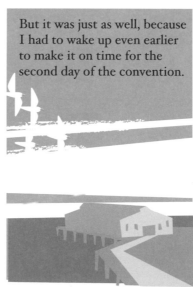

"Ugh!"

Fin

Plus One

Along with New Year's, Christmas, Valentine's Day, even-numbered birthdays, and let's face it, mornings in general, weddings seem to bring out the worst in me.

There's nothing worse than being forced to bear witness to two happy people,--

--making me reflective about how unhappy I am in my own life.

It isn't the idea of long term relationships that bother me.

I have had more than my share of failed relationships to prove to myself that being in or coming out of one fills me with neither fear nor disinterest,--

And it isn't the idea of going into financial hardship to celebrate this bond, because I have become quite accustomed to being perpetually broke.

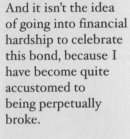

I think what bothers me about weddings is that they symbolize a very particular stage in life,--

--that I don't think I would be ever able to achieve,--

-- a proper adulthood.

But for some reason, at least twice every summer since I had entered my mid twenties,--

--weddings had become as expected and about as welcome an event as finding another gray hair on my head.

But it's worse when you don't know either the bride nor the groom well.

A girlfriend of mine, Julia, asked me in a panic to come with her to one.

She had a been nursing a crush on the best man, Andy.

I couldn't blame her-he was gorgeous.

Andy had started dating a new girl recently and Julia wasn't taking it well.

So once again, I found myself in the awkward position of being a friend's plus one.

Recently I had been adopted by a new circle of much younger of which both Julia and Andy were a part.

They all seemed a bit awkward and lost, so naturally I fit right in.

Over the years, I had slowly lost contact with many friends whose lives seemed to be going toward either career or family,--

Admittedly, I had little interest in either.

Consequently, out of sheer loneliness, I more than happily overlooked the odd age descrepancy and started hanging around them more and more.

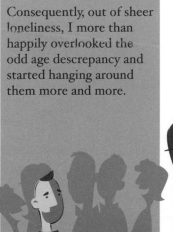

Perhaps it was because they were all about fifteen years younger than me,--

--that in my state of arrested development, I related to them so well.

While providing emotional support for Julia, I nursed my own crush.

His name was Peter. To be honest, I was a bit confused about why I was even interested in him.

He wasn't exactly my type. He smoked and drank way too much, he didn't dress well, and he wasn't ambitious in any way. His personality was completely opposite of my own.

People tell me I remind them of a cat. Peter was just the opposite, a friendly pup.

But we got along famously and often found ourselves chatting over drinks and cigarettes until well into the morning, engrossed in conversation.

I suppose when two people spend as much time together as we did, emotional attachments are inevitable.

Of course, he knew about my odd crush on him.

I'm pretty transparent when it comes to things like that, but he never seemed to take interest.

74

I suppose that is why I agreed to go to the wedding with Julia.

In rejection, I had felt a kinship with her.

But as uncomfortable as I was to be at that wedding emotionally, I was even more ill at ease physically.

I don't know why people choose summer for their weddings.

What makes a sweltering afternoon in the middle of July an appropriate time to wear a three-piece suit?

And why didn't anyone else look as visibly uncomfortable as I must have looked?

So between dealing with the puddle of sweat slowly collecting in my trousers,--

--keeping check on Julia's angrily darting eyes at Andy's date,--

--and my own distraction with Peter,--

--I heard the foreboding whistle of disaster like the moment right before a train wreck.

The reception was held at the groom's childhood home in a rather well to do part of San Marino.

And tensions seemed to ease as the afternoon rolled along.

Honestly, I think plying everyone with food and drinks is the best form of social lubricant.

Julia bravely introduced herself to Andy's date and discovered they had a good deal in common.

Later she would confess to me,--

"Honestly, it would all be a bit too easy to hate her.
But she's actually pretty cool. Ugh, why did she have to be so cool?"

I was proud of her. She showed a lot more maturity than I would have.

I would have been crying in my soup by now.

I was into my second beer, but Peter was already drunk and busy flirting with every guy there,--

--except me.

I was almost certain that he was going out of his way to avoid me.

I didn't know why, since he had known about my crush on him for months.

Peter was in really bad shape.

Near the end of the evening, I found him slumped alone on the sidewalk. I sat next to him.

"Hey, are you all right?

Let's get you back inside and sober you up."

Uncharacteristically, Peter angrily barked,—

"Stay away from me!"

In a drunken slur, he then sneered something about anthrax.

I never found out just what it was about me that Peter found so unappealing,—

—but if that rant was any indication of what he really thought of me romantically, it was best to simply not know at all.

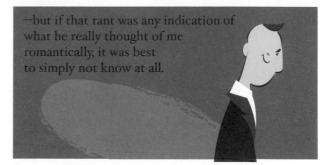

In an effort to cool off from the heat and nurse my bruised ego,--

--I stole away inside and decided to hide out in the restroom.

By now, what I'm assuming had started out as modest sweat rings under my suit,--

--had formed into voluminous puddles somehow venting an impossible amount of their own heat not unlike a geyser.

"Oh God, it's so moist! Everything's so MOIST!"

I took some toilet paper in a futile attempt to dry off.

When it flushed down in an odd slow swirl, I thought,--

...glug...

"Hmm, --

"--maybe one more flush for good measure. I don't want to be blamed for clogging up the toilet."

When I flushed the toilet a second time,--

-- it began to overflow.

"Oh God, Oh God, Oh God!"

In my panic, I had forgotten all about the supply valve, which I would normally turn off in situations like this,--

"Oh God, Oh God, Oh God!"

Instead, I reached for a set of guest towels to sop up the slowly flooding hardwood floor.

"Oh God, Oh God, Oh God!"

Thankfully, I managed to find a plunger and made quick work of cleaning up the mess.

I then decided to hide all evidence of my crime behind the shower curtain.

When I came out, a line had formed waiting to use the restroom.

Surely they all knew what I did...

79

It was then that Andy spotted me.

"That's where you've been! We've been looking everywhere for you!"

"We all figured you were hiding out to avoid dancing."

Then, in a familial show of affection, he placed his arm around me—

—as if to insure that I would not escape him and guided me to the dance floor.

"Geez, how hot are you right now?"

"I can feel you radiating heat through your jacket!"

"Hey, where's Julia? I haven't seen her for half the night?"

"Oh, you're not going to believe who she's talking to."

Fin

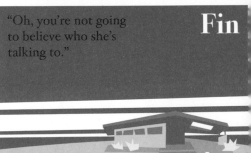

I have this ongoing joke with a friend of mine, that if we could have any one magical item,--

--it would be a wand--

--that turns anyone you point to gay.

Of course, if I were to actually have this wand, it wouldn't make my life anymore different than it is already,--

--because anyone who I would transform would almost certainly tell me,--

"Sorry, you're not my type."

The gay world is divided into different types of guys but, unfortunately for me,--

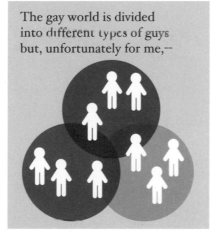

Nobody's Type

I don't seem to fit into any one of these categories.

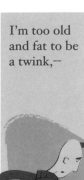I'm too old and fat to be a twink,--

--and not fat enough to be a chub,--

--not fit enough to be a jock,--

--too young to consider myself anyone's daddy,--

--and I'm definitely not hairy enough to be a bear or otter.

It makes filling out online dating forms difficult if you don't seem to relate to any descriptors they give you for their profiles.

How can I find anyone if I don't seem to fit--

-- the gay world's exaggerated sexual ideals?

Where's the box that I can check?

Where is the space for me?

Things become even more complicated when race is entered into the equation.

I'm not Asian-looking enough to attract guys who are into Asians,--

--and not Latino-looking enough for guys who are into Latinos.

Sadly, I have come across more racism in the gay world than anywhere else.

From the mildly offensive,--

"I don't usually go for Asians, but you're kind of hot."

--to the downright offensive,--

"Ugh, Asian and Latinos are horrible. They smell like garlic."

I find it sad when I meet someone who strictly limits himself to one particular type of guy. "Sorry, I don't do Asians- you are Asian aren't you? I can't really tell."

"Yeah, I only date black twinks."

In polite circles, statements like these are often either prefaced or followed with the words "No offense,"--

--which of course I take as a polite way of saying something offensive.

Neither heavy, thin, muscled, average nor age or race ever seemed to be an issue for me.

So what does that mean when you like all kinds of men? Does that make me virtuous or just a slut?

Thus, my entire dating life has been a bit backwards.

Instead of trying to figure out what I am looking for in a relationship,--

--I seem to stumble from one random guy to another--

--hoping I fit somehow into someone's ideal.

But I thought I had left that behind me when I met Justyn.

Unlike a lot of guys who I had dated in the past, our interests seemed to complement each other;--

--music, art, design, food.

We were both dreamers and spent a lot of time planning our lives together.

He was more than just a boyfriend, he was a partner professionally as well.

Someone who not only got excited about my art as much as I did, but who wanted to work on it with me as well.

He used to send me sweet little messages constantly--

"I love you."

In fact, it was the first time anyone had ever said that to me.

That's why it was a shock when he told me one day,–

"I cheated on you."

The only thing I could think was,–

"Who are you?"

After almost two years together, I thought I knew everything about him.

"I still love you."

I didn't hear much of anything he told me afterwards, it all sounded insincere.

I stopped seeing him.

It wasn't until three months later, after the death of a mutual friend, that we started talking to each other again.

I thought we were on the road to reconciliation.

It was months before he told me yet again,–

"I'm seeing someone else."

I reacted a bit differently this time: I was mad.

Angry that yet again he had been keeping secrets from me,--

--I pressed him why,--

"I just don't find you attractive anymore.
I want a hairy Latino."

"In fact, I don't think I ever really loved you."

I had forgiven him for his first indiscretion.

In fact I would have been okay with an open relationship if he had just been honest with me.

But one thing that I could never forgive Justyn for--

--was taking back his love for me.

I ended up erasing all his contact information on both my computer and phone--

--and told him I never wanted to see him again.

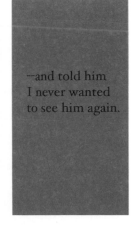

But I couldn't bear to erase the little messages he used to send.

When I open them up to read them, they don't have Justyn's name on them anymore.

They are simply reduced to anonymous love letters to myself.

I'm not sure why I bothered to keep them,—

—I guess it's a hopeful reminder that somewhere I will find someone who will tell me those words again,—

—but next time, mean it.

Fin

You don't normally think of time as something larger than yourself. After all, it is portioned out in minutes-but it can be huge.

One day I woke up and I realized, I had been dating for twenty years.

Twenty years.

It's hard to imagine anyone with as little resolve as I have, doing anything for so long.

And despite all my efforts, after all that time, I find myself single again.

loveline

headline

lifeline

In any other endeavor by now, most people would simply pack and give up.

After all, what says failure more than twenty years of effort?

Baggage

So when should I give up?

With each year that passes, little by little, I can see the youth slip from my face.

And I sense a slow swell of urgency that manifests as a rumbling in my gut. My time, which once seemed so abundant, is running out.

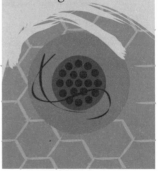

My friends are getting to the point in their lives where they are settling down and having kids. In many ways I feel like I'm getting left behind. I've always been slow out of the gate and catching up is all I seem to do.

But it seems that the longer I stay single, I see that same point for me gets further and further away.

I used to keep old boyfriends around as friends, I saw it as a sign of emotional maturity.

But over the years, I've found keeping them around to be a needless complication.

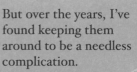

Despite my best efforts, they tend to hang around in other ways.

They linger in my mind as stray thoughts.

And over the years, I've developed quite a collection.

These days, I I can't seem to shake them.

Their faces pop up around the city like landmarks.

LA has become a mosaic of my failed relationships.

Until recently, I've never understood why people feel compelled to uproot their lives for something new.

As I drive, I recollect old conversations and arguments.

My exes haunt me like ghosts.

They follow me everywhere.

I recently went on a date with Todd, a longtime online acquaintance.

We'd known each other for years,--

--but for some reason our timing to meet in person had always been off.

Upon seeing him for the first time, I wondered what he was even doing there with me.

Todd was ridiculously good-looking,--

--so much so that a wave of self-conciousness came over me.

I began to look around to gauge the reaction of others on how we looked together.

Todd was way out of my league,--

--and I wondered if it was obvious to anyone else but me.

I was pretty much my usual self: fidgety, nervous, and awkward.

I can only guess what Todd was thinking of me.

There's a general rule with first dates: don't talk about your exes. It is pretty much a red flag for emotional unavailability.

But in my nervousness, I couldn't help myself and out came story after story about one ex and then another.

It's like my mouth and my head were disconnected.

My past had become an inescapable behemoth haunting me from here on in.

Is this what they mean by having baggage?

All the years of dating finally caught up with me.

93

After years of chats filled with flirting,--

--we parted ways in an awkward, sexless hug.

I sat in the parking lot to collect my thoughts, stewing about where I went wrong.

Todd passed me by in his sedan without as much as a wave of his hand.

Clearly, this date wouldn't be haunting him tonight.

I'm sure he was just grateful to be going.

Oddly, enough, for the first time that night,--

--I felt truly alone, free of any ghosts.

Sadly, the only thing I have to show for all my years of dating are my ghosts.

I can feel them around like a phantom limb.

Whenever a relationship ends, I feel like I've left something behind.

Or more likely something is taken away.

After twenty years of dating, I'm not sure much of me has been left behind.

What could I possibly bring to a relationhip in this state?

With age, I can reconcile my past with increasing clarity.

But the problem with history is that it is cumulative and eventually, it becomes overwhelmingly crowded.

Sometimes, like on awkward first dates,--

--when I can't seem to shut up about my exes,--

--it's like a curse.

But my past does provide me with a good deal of perspective.

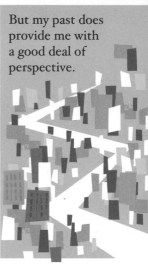

I can't say I know what I want, but at least I know what I don't.

And obviously, I still don't know what I'm doing.

But it's like a second date,--

--with the extra experience, I can at least get by looking a bit more confident.

Fin